The Healing of Me

Lisa Scovell-Strickland

MY DREAMS

Which path to choose
To redefine my dreams
A dream once remembered clear
Lays distorted between pay checks
Backwards motion but forwards thinking
Stalemate once more
To give a little, may get a little
But is it really enough?
To dream what I want, or
To have what I dream of

First published in 2025 by
Stone Phoenix Press in collaboration with Lemon Jelly Press
Isle of Wight
UK
PO36 0LL

Copyright lies with the author.
All rights reserved. No part of this publication can be reproduced, stored in a retrieval system, or transmitted in any form or by any means, electronic, mechanical, photocopying, recoding or otherwise, without prior permission of the publishers.

This publication is sold subject to the condition that it shall not, by way of trade or otherwise, be lent, re-sold, hired out or otherwise circulated without the publisher's prior consent in any form of binding or cover other than that which it is published and without a similar condition including this condition being imposed on the subsequent purchaser.

ISBN 978-1-7395415-1-4
Cover design by Olivia Johansson
find her on Instagram @viajohansson_paints

Acknowledgements

Sometimes saying thank you seems woefully inadequate. Nevertheless, I thank those who have made the most impact on my healing journey:

My high school teachers Claire and Trish, who despite the backdrop of Section 28, created a supportive environment for me whilst I navigated the rollercoaster of accepting myself when the world around me was not so kind.

My beautiful wife Zara, who picked me up when I fell and supported me until I could stand upon my own again.

My chosen family, Annette, Darren, Emily and Olivia. Who have always accepted me for the way I am, without question. Olivia, I am in awe of your incredible talent and I am so honoured to have your work adorn the front cover of this collection. I am so proud of you and all of what you have yet to achieve.

My cheerleaders, Charlotte and Tracy whose own strength and resilience helped me when I needed it most.

My Cameo Stranger for their continuing support, kind words; and word prompts which encourage me to step out of my writing comfort zone.

BEFORE I RELEASED MY WORDS

I had kept these words to myself, some for a long time
Some of them had decades of dust upon them
I dusted the older ones off
Lined them up with the new ones
I noticed the patterns with similar emotions repeating
I considered their relevance to others
I questioned whether others would be able to relate to me
The words were so much a part of me
Tattooed to my skin in invisible ink
Embedded in my heart, regulating its rhythm
Whirling in my mind, never allowing it to calm
Sewn into the fabric of me, holding me together
I wondered if I would lose a part of me should I set them free
I ruminated on the idea of their release
Then pondered some more on what it meant to me
After which I overanalysed and scrutinised each word I had written
Trying to estimate each barrier that would prevent me from shouting them out to the world
After a while, I came to the conclusion
That the only barrier was my fear
So, I dug deep for my courage
Slowly drip fed them out in batches
First to close friends and loved ones

Then to a cameo stranger
To my surprise the words landed
Parallels were made, emotions were shared
Connections were formed, cheerleaders were gained
All this so quickly became comfortable
As I realised, I didn't need to be afraid
Because it's words that bind us together
It just needs someone to start the conversation
By being brave enough to speak the first word

CONTENTS

THE HEALING OF ME...1-2
AFTER I RELEASED THE WORDS......................................3-4
STANDING ON THE EDGE OF REMEMBRANCE LOOKING AT THE VIEW...5-6
WARRIOR QUEEN..7
STARTING AGAIN...8
EYES LIKE MINE..9-10
OVERWHELMED..11-12
STRONG AND BRAVE...13-14
GRADUATION..15-16
SHACKLES...17
THE ETERNAL SPRINGTIME...18
SPRING..19
THE ETERNAL SPRINGTIME NO. 2...20
SUMMER..21
UNTITLED..22
DAYSPRING...23
EVENTIDE..24
GREEN FINGERS..25
THE JOURNEY..26
HINDSIGHT IS MY JAILER NO MORE...............................27-28
SELENE...29
THE WIELDING OF MY WORDS...30
I SHED TEARS UNDER THE LIGHT OF THE MOON..31-12
PERFECT WEEKEND...33-34
MORNING REVERENCE..35
SOLITUDE...36

SILENCE	37
WRITING	38
DANCING IN MY LIVING ROOM	39-40
THOSE FIRST WAKING MOMENTS BEFORE I START THE DAY	41-42
SERENITY	43
COASTAL ADVENTURES	44
MINDFULNESS	45-46
THE COMFORT OF YOUR EMBRACE	47
COMPETENCY	48
AS LOVERS MEET AGAIN	49
THE CALM BETWEEN THE WORDS	50
SANCTUARY	51
SKIN TO SKIN	52
THE WHISPER OF YOUR VOICE	53
A LITTLE THANK YOU	54
LET MY WORDS ROAM FREE	55-56
DRIFTING TOWARDS SOMETHING NEW	57-58
PATH TO FREEDOM	59
FINDING MY IDENTITY	60-61
WHISPERS AND REMEMBERANCE	62
WORDS FROM YOUR CHEERLEADER	63

THE HEALING OF ME

I thought that once I rose as a Phoenix
That all my sins would be washed away
With the darkness trapped never to return again
It wasn't this simple
The healing of me will always be in progress
As I strip away decades of self-hatred embedded in my skin
Quiet the voices in my head with my burning affirmations
As I line up my cheerleaders to counsel me
Banishing the naysayers from my inner circle
I may have to rise the Phoenix many times
Root out the evil within my ranks, shuffling the pack
I may have to rewrite my affirmations to make them stick
But I will do this for myself again and again
For as long at it takes
With my head held high
My Warrior Queen mantra becomes my battle cry
As I heal my wounds
Cleanse myself in new waters
Baptise myself in the warmth of my love

Remembering that the darkness stands only two steps to my left
Just in reach
So I keep stepping right
Lit by the warmth of a thousand new days
Protected by Selene and her silver night light
Knowing that I am
The Phoenix
The Warrior Queen
I have fallen
I have risen
I put myself back together
Sealing those wounds with love
Ready to cherish the heart of me
Ready to start living
Ready to light the way for others
Taking one day at a time

AFTER I RELEASED MY WORDS

The first thing I noticed was the noise subsided
My inner sound system dialed down several decibels
Whilst sharing the words I had written to my cheerleaders had stilled my mind
When I finally spoke those words to the room
It's space filled with my chosen family, friends, new faces
I wasn't quite prepared for such inner calm
I should have been glad of this
It was what I wanted all along
To be able to exist comfortably
In my own skin
My mind clear
But initially I panicked as no comfort came
As I had held on too long to all those words
They comforted me with negative emotions
The darkness that lingered
The pain that burnt my soul
But I carried on speaking each word with unpractised ease
I began to understand that I had wrapped myself in the wrong words
Compounding my suffering by clinging to what had come before

And now I had released them all
As each word spilled from my lips
I experienced the strangest feelings
Hope for brighter days
The promise of new connections, opportunities
An inner calm, not numbness
I could feel my narrative rewriting itself
Etching my affirmations across my skin
Absorbing them into my grey matter
I had found the key to unlock myself
As I stood there reading the last poem
For the first time I felt truly me
I smiled, because I had allowed myself to be free

STANDING ON THE EDGE OF REMEMBRANCE LOOKING AT THE VIEW

I find myself standing on that edge again
But this time I am not here to start anew
I'm here to look back
To review and take stock
Ruminate and highlight
Celebrate and commiserate
All the milestones which got me to this precipice
My head still held high
As I catalogue it all
The positive and the negative
The unpretty and the beautiful
All the times I picked myself up to start again
The moments when giving up seemed the smartest option
The happy times when things were going so well I could have burst open in colours
The dark times when it took my light and hid it from the world and myself
The in between times when I was so numb I was barely alive in the world
I list all those connections, the ones…
I have lost and I have made
I have loved and sometimes hated
I have been afraid of
I have laughed with until I cried

And as I think of those tears...
The happy ones and the sad ones
The dry ones and the extra wet ones
I realise, I could fill an ocean with them and still not run out
I use those tears to cleanse myself
The saltiness healing all my wounds
Ever so slowly but surely
I listen to my heart beat, slow and steady
Grateful that I let it keep beating
Knowing it sustains me with each beat
Hugging myself tightly, I feel the love for myself, from myself which I finally acknowledge as a privilege
The culmination of letting go and peeling back those negative layers which I allowed others to shroud me within
A sigh of relief escapes my lips, my heart full
My head mercifully quiet
Comfortable in the afternoon sun
I come to the conclusion that
I am doing ok
I am healing at my own pace
In my own time
Because this what I finally know I deserve
Something I have waited for a very long time
Which is finally in my sights as I take in the view

WARRIOR QUEEN

I stand here soaked in sweat
Knuckles raw, limbs bruised
My training partner slammed into the mat
And all I can think of is those faces
The eyes of each of them, some blurry
They all tried to take something from me
Each of them took a little souvenir
As I lost a little piece of me inside
That was replaced with silent fear
Now as I force air into my lungs
My chest burning from the exertion
My power drained from the force I used
My skin vibrating with energy
I replace that with
Strength
Fortitude
Determination
My mantra as a Warrior Queen

STARTING AGAIN

Vibrations between my erratic heartbeats
Just a microsecond between each beat
Between my inhale and exhale
Introductions are made
As my uncertain glance finds kind eyes
Locked in fresh understanding of where I am at this moment

Like a moth to a flame I cannot help but gravitate towards that understanding
Knowing that it will render me vulnerable
An open book on display for all to see
But the sanctuary it offers
The salvation it promises
Shows me that this safe space is what I needed

I keep our eyes locked as I share my trauma past and present
Ready to learn the positive ways to soothe myself
Open to the learning and growth that awaits
Determined to find the best of me buried so deep in the darkness
Anxious that my rebirth may not stick
Committed to the journey that lies ahead

EYES LIKE MINE

When I looked at their faces, I felt like the odd one out
Generations apart from them
Language barriers and cultural differences
So I smiled genuinely
I spoke honestly
Ordering my words with care
And when they allowed me in
That is when I saw it
Embedded in every face I met
They had eyes like mine
I'm not talking about the colour
Although occasionally this was true
I mean the things unspoken that reside in one's eyes
Silently communicated until given the opportunity to be voiced
Or the courage is built to speak the words
So I let them speak
I let them spill their truths
Set out their dreams
Talk about their troubles and fears
The more they talked, the more I felt the need to comfort them
Guide them towards the positive
Reassure them that the pain won't always last
I shared my words

My truths
    My struggles
        My triumphs
            My affirmations

As it became apparent that all they needed
Was to share their darkness, so it could be conquered together
To be seen in the wake of their truths
No matter how disturbing they believed themselves to be
To be heard in their authentic voices
Without the fear of judgement or sanction
But above all they just wanted to be connected to those around them
To belong to something where they could be their own truths in whatever medium they wanted
And I love them all for that
Because I feel the same, I want the same things
For whilst I may be further along the path
I may be at a different waypoint
My journey is the same
And I am happy to pause mine to guide them when they need it
Since they will also help me further along my path
All the fuller and brighter for having made the connection

OVERWHELMED

I sit in the eye of it all
Stunned still, rooted to the spot
My head snaps left and right of its own accord
My ears buzzing with static and the tune of a merry go round
I close my eyes thinking this will help
But it just makes the spinning in my head more violent and out of control
My neck clicks, the pressure popping the air right out of the joints
A loud pop…crunch
I thought this time that my head would come clean off
I am detached from my body
I do not feel my limbs twitch
I sense a hand on my shoulder
It burns and I try to shy away
I hear a voice, muffled like it is underwater
I make out my name, but that is all
My blood is pumping so hard it replaces the static in my ears
The hand is at my shoulder again
And this time I lash out violently
GET OFF ME, I hear the words spill from my mouth
The voice just about sounds like me
But it wasn't said aloud, it was in my head
I realise I hadn't moved
Fear glued my limbs together

My mind tricked me into thinking that I had fought back against that old threat
My breath stutters and I can barely catch it
That's when I hear a calm voice
Slowly saying my name
Asking me to count back from ten
Gently rubbing my hands in circles
Anti-clockwise I think
As the spinning slows down
The static starts to subside
I start to take deeper breaths
Feeling my limbs loosen gently
Awareness creeping back in
Stunned to discover that it was my calm voice from the back of my mind
It was my right hand soothing my left one, reviving me
I start to feel the shame of losing my composure, my control
But I remember what triggers this
And all I need to focus on is that I survived
I am stronger than before
As I keep fighting for myself everyday

STRONG AND BRAVE

I know that you always question yourself

What more could you have done?
Could you have spoken up sooner?
What if you had done something different would the outcome have been the same?

If only you had made a different choice

Would you have chosen a different path?
What if you had used other words?
What if you had let them in, just once?

These are thoughts that consume you over and over
Until you spiral in upon yourself
Running through scenarios that aren't even plausible
But still your heart and your head run them in tandem
It will be the questions and thoughts that consume you on the dark days
Focusing you in the wrong direction
When you need to look forwards
Preparing yourself for what is to come

Remember that despite what has come before you can only affect the future
Embrace the challenge of meeting the future full on
In the knowledge that you will always be prepared
Even if you are not, you have the resilience to face any challenge
Courage burns deep in your soul
Fortitude burns brightly in your eyes
Remember that you have overcome adversity time and time again
Remember that you are strong and brave

GRADUATION

As I don my gown, cap and hood for the third time in my life
I reflect on the hard work that led to this day
Over two years I studied hard to Master my knowledge and skills
Starting this journey amidst the period that the world was turned upside down
When we had to protect ourselves from each other and vice versa
Our connections became distant and virtual
I learnt to maintain a work /study balance unlike anything I had achieved before
My work / life balance had become a distant memory
My studies grounded me from the realities of trying to keep my community safe
They gave me a sense of purpose for what my future would hold
They reminded me that I am capable, resilient and confident even when I think I am not
As I was shuffled in lines amongst all the other graduates I could feel the pride vibrating in the air
The smiles unforced and jubilation clear on each and every face I met
The anticipation of those few minutes of being the centre of the universe for each of us

The nervousness about that walk across the stage, don't trip!
The proud cheerleaders we all had to watch our special moment
A tinge of sadness for those of us who had absent cheerleaders
And all at once my moment came as I strode out to roaring applause
In this moment my smile grew so big I could barely contain it
Pride swelled deep within the very core of me
As I shook the hands of congratulations I whispered to myself
Look what you have achieved
Be proud
Remember this moment
For whilst it may be fleeting
Everything that led to this will be with you always

SHACKLES

I rub my wrists and ankles where those imaginary bindings used to be
My movement now so fluid and free
Not realising how much I had held myself back
How small I had become
Through fear
Self loathing
Sadness
Darkness
The all consuming pain of everything I denied myself
My mind shackled by my emotions
My spirit shackled by the words of others
I can see now how much I have missed out on
As my shackles made me retreat into myself
Kept me locked in and muted
When I could have embraced all that I was and wanted to be
But I cannot dwell on this
I must look forward
Allow myself to be free of all that came before
So that those shackles remain a memory of the girl I used to be
As I embrace the woman I have become

THE ETERNAL SPRINGTIME

Slipped between the seasons
Not yet in bloom, not yet alive
After cruel sleep, after dark
Waiting in silence, revealing their waking dreams
Sleepy heads unwind, stretching their full potential
Slowly shifting as spring blooms once more
Fragile beginnings unfold under the light of dawn
As wonderous scents seduce the innocent
Dreams rise above the shadowy water of doubt
Many loves blossom this time and stay forever

SPRING

Today the sun has flushed my soul
As gentle breezes chase my disquiet
I breathe in silent relief
And out with deafening expectancy
Such renewal brings forth jubilance to mine eyes
Sweet melodies of colour sing
As blooms burst in naked wonder
Heady scents chase me
I close the door to my secret garden
I sit decidedly, and soak it all in
As I take a pleasant sojourn in solitude

THE ETERNAL SPRINGTIME NO. 2

Like a cold day in January
The new year and old habits put to rest
The flowers of spring yet to bloom
Other father time keeps turning, whilst
Old mother earth watches with patience
As old seeds spread, and young shoots grow
The water of life drops gently upon each new beginning
As the eternal springtime wakes again

SUMMER

An army of butterflies at my door
Regiments of colour fluttering in the sun
A source of amusement
A scene of beauty and grace
They dance in the breeze
Settle on nature's honey
Flip flap of their wings
Silent, yet determined
I watch in awe of the rainbow
And wait for summer's next display

UNTITLED

There was a pre-spring interlude as I wandered today
Through verdant fields, muddy puddles
Across undulating cliffs
Leading waggy tails, whose noses sought out
Mischief in the undergrowth

I, captivated by spring's smile
Stepping down to the shore
Sea spray tickled my cheeks
Waves thundered against the revetment
Relentless and rhythmic

Here I could finally breathe
The fog in my mind lifted
Struck by mine own clarity
I was reminded by Vectis that
"All this beauty is of god"

DAYSPRING

Today's potential rises slowly before me
Unveiling hues of pink and gold and blue
Which backlight a line of resolute oaks
A sentry guard to the paradise valley
I gaze in awe at the spectacular of the unfolding scene
My senses fit to burst with wonder
Songs of renewal sung by early birds
Fill my ears and echo through the trees
I stand awhile witnessing the sublime
Before I turn inspired once again

EVENTIDE

I walk our circular route for the final time
Ruminating on the hubbub of this very day
The light fading amid a golden glow
I chase the last warm embers it projects
Conversations had, replayed in black and white
Opportunities missed, highlighted in dazzling effulgence
My mind all of a pother at my procrastination
Twinkling lights appear in the gloaming, as vesper service chimes
I am reminded that I can begin tomorrow anew in earnest

GREEN FINGERS

My fingers prepare the soil
Cool to the touch, but warming
Bursting with potential
I plan out this season's produce
Planting by numbers
Not always by design
Splashes of colour here and there
Satisfaction over my toil
I sit back and admire
Categorising what is where
Now I wait
To see what makes the surface
Ready to nurture it all to fruition

THE JOURNEY

Sitting across from my beautiful
Sipping coffee and gazing out of the window
The train trundles to a station stop
Sunlight bathes us in warmth
As we read across the table from each other
I sneak a glance over my book
Watching her as she reads intently
Captivated by her latest genre
I study her closely
Those green eyes soaking in every word
Micro frowns turn to smiles at a section she finds amusing
She catches me and holds my gaze
Her eyes soften and we share a secret smile
I try to convey all my love for her
Wishing I could reach over to kiss her lips
She takes a deep breath, returns to her book
And whispers, "love you to the moon and back"
Smiling, I turn to the window flushed with emotion
And quietly take in the view

HINDSIGHT IS MY JAILER NO MORE

I sometimes ponder whether I want to go back
Travel back to when I first noticed the pain
To hold my hand and tell me not to worry
That the darkness won't take me away
But it would shape me, mould me into something strong
Or would I want to go back
To prevent those times when someone else's darkness took me, shook me and left me broken
Give me the skills to defend myself against those faces who so desperately wanted to possess me
Would it have made a difference?
Would knowing what was to come have changed my actions?
Altered the path I was set upon?
Given me a happier, brighter journey?
I tell myself I cannot deal in the what ifs, or the maybes
The would haves or the should haves
Don't talk to me about the could haves
Hindsight, oh wonderfully wicked hindsight
It had become my jailer
It had locked me in my negative state

Doomed me to replay the worst bits, the darkest times
I looped back and forth and round and round
Trying to reach a different outcome
Each time I only came back to the truth of what happened on those days, during those times
For despite my need to fix me
Right the wrongs that were done to me
Stop me from the wrongs I did to myself
I know deep down that I won't, I can't, I shouldn't
For everything that has happened
Shaped me, created the woman before you today
The woman who stands here stronger than ever
The woman who has learnt to love herself again
The woman who without all that came before, could never be the same

SELENE

I watched you as you rose last night
Full of splendour and promise
I've known you by many names
Only one personifies your beauty
You command the tides
A beacon in the dark
Cyclical and transcendental
I worship your phases
I rest in your crescent
As you watch over my slumber

THE WIELDING OF MY WORDS

I don't have the strength to keep all the negativity away
So I force myself to look the other way
Turn the other cheek to focus on all the good, warm and positive that comes my way
I minimise myself to make the target smaller
Give them less to aim for but that doesn't last long
And I ask myself, why am I hardwired this way?
Why does the negative outweigh the positive?
Why do the criticisms, the cold shoulders and the open attacks cut deeper and quicker?
I think of all the words I have inside me
The negative ones that I have received from others or told myself
I realise that these will be my armour
They will be my shield
I will wield them as my sword
For the words no longer control me like they used to
Now I control them

I SHED TEARS UNDER THE LIGHT OF THE MOON

As I gaze up to Selene in all her glory
I feel the unshed tears dusting my eyelashes
My emotions have been so out of sorts today
From happy to sad to angry and every scale in between
But mostly sad and angry
Disappointment greeted by false hope
I wish I knew what you were thinking
Where I stood in your tableau vivant
Am I the blessed child you embrace tightly
Or am I the dark sheep cast out for fear of corrupting the rest of the flock
I try to push away such negativity
Wanting to give you the time to come to me of your own accord
Even though I realise this is wishful thinking
I cannot help but court hope fervently
I hold my head in my hands and let go
Let those tears map the surface of my face
Tracking down my cheeks, my chin
Spilling downwards, releasing all my emotions at once
My silent sobs caught by the moonlight

The Healing of Me | Lisa Scovell-Strickland

I hear Selene whisper to me gently
That despite this all, I am blessed
With the love of others who value me for all my worth
I catch my breaths until they become even again
Feeling the light of Selene fill my dark corners
Pouring into me such love and positivity
Reminding me that I should be proud of who I am
Of who I am yet to be
Of who I was before
I shiver as the night's breeze hits me
I stand tall, renewed by her light
Climbing the stairs in search of slumber

PERFECT WEEKEND

This weekend I caught up with my chosen family
We spent time foraging the hedgerows for sweet treats
Our waggy tails sniffing out each berry
We laughed and laughed basking in our respect and love for each other
As we wished the summer would last longer

My beautiful and I took the waggy tails wandering
Enjoying the company of good friends
The opportunity to coo over the youngest family member
A chance to savour the joy of amusing such innocence with funny faces and a make shift drum
These moments were so wonderful to capture
Connections being renewed and bonds being strengthened further

However, the most cherished moments to pass were the most simple
My beautiful and I, our hands working the soil, harvesting the veg and sowing new seeds
Taking care of the garden for its next phase in the cycle
Whilst at the same time taking care of ourselves, and each other
Connecting with nature, reminding us that we stay grounded in it
That the more we immerse ourselves in it, the healthier we become

The waggy tails trying to help in all the wrong places
Noses where they shouldn't be

I can still taste the meal we cooked together towards the end of the day
A culinary delight which was made with the love we have for each other
Precious time on the sofa, sharing each other's space
The waggy tails cuddled in
Providing a soundtrack to the silence with their snuffly-snores

As we climbed the stairs to slumber land
We felt the aching of our limbs from our labour
The heaviness of them so comforting, a welcome decompression
And as we lay in each other's arms
Feeling the pull of sleep overcome us
I whispered, this has been the perfect weekend
Hoping that in our future there would be many more to come

MORNING REVERENCE

My Norse gods and I wander round our usual routes
Their waggy tails chasing their noses
As they strut in awe of a new day
We soak in the morning sun
Its rays tentative but warming
They embrace the opportunities to sniff out the other locals
Taking in the fresh air, we come to the end of our jaunt
Settling onto the sofa
Bathed in the morning light
They cuddle into me
We take a moment to reflect
Before they fall into slumber peacefully

SOLITUDE

I crave solitude
Sometimes more than the embrace of others
I seek a place to rest with my thoughts and feelings
To work through my troubles
Or quietly celebrate my personal triumphs of the day
It won't matter if it is day or night
But it has to be outside
Where I can ground myself in nature
Touch the bark of the tree feeling it's sage roughness wondering what it has witnessed during its tenure
Tickle the leaf of the ferns watching them unfurl in spring and brown in autumn
Soaking in the colours of the flowers, blossoms and the beautiful sky at any time of the day or year
Gazing at the night sky trying to work out where Cassiopeia resides at that moment
It won't matter to me if it rains as I let this wash over me
Cleanse me as if part of a sacred ritual
What matters to me is that I am given the space to take this time for myself
So I can return the favour once my self-care is complete

SILENCE

Today I reached a point I never thought I would
The day that I found silence in my head
An inner calm befell me
It was roughly half past four
As I came home full of happiness
Walked through the front door
My wife took me into her embrace
Whispering in my ear 'I'm so proud of you'
Earlier I had had my heart in my mouth
It's beating echoing in my ears
I pouring words out of me to strangers in the room
My words being transmitted far and wide
Now I feel empty but full all at once
Another weight lifted from my chest
Another new challenge met
I quite like this silence and I hope it stays awhile

WRITING

A moment of inspiration
Within the hallowed mind of me
Retro thinking its outspoken
Whispers silently in my ear
No real thought or reason
Just a jumble of words forming
Through mind over matter
In sickness and health
Writings on the page
On the wall, black and white
Painted on the clouds
As my spotless mind requested
Still no rhyme or reason
They just fall out from my mind
Stream of something else
Waiting for some purpose
Till the river runs dry
And echoes fill my ears

DANCING IN MY LIVING ROOM

A little treat just for me
In a moment that I get to call my own
I start the music
Let the beat catch me
Feeling it rush to me
Invade my senses
Take hold
I begin to sway
My body overtaken
With joy
A love of life
My movements fluid
Without thought
Just letting the beat
Dictate my shapes
Form my silhouette
My breaths long and deep
Inhaling sound
Exhaling colours
I feel myself centre
At one with every fibre of my being

I feel freedom
My eyes closed
Feeling my way instinctively
I let the notes and words
Wash over me
Vibrate through me
I am beautifully wasted
On the tempo
With the beats
Consumed by the rhythm of it all
I feel endlessly connected
To everything around me
My skin sparkles
My eyes golden
Knowing this euphoria
Will last for hours

THOSE FIRST WAKING MOMENTS BEFORE I START THE DAY

There are precious few moments
That I like to savour more than this
In the early hours of the morning
When the birds are singing to bring the day break
As I slowly wake, stretching sedately
I find myself between slumber and consciousness
Warm fuzzy thoughts emanating from me
The feel of your love enveloping me
As you hold me tight in your embrace
I open one eye cautiously
Wanting to resist the inevitable start of the day
Wanting to prevent my mind bolting out of the start gate
And hurtle through every negative thought I currently manage
I want to remain in this warm glow for as long as possible
Let the radiance of the August sun soak into my soul
As it peaks through the gap in the drapes
I focus on my breaths, deep and steady
Hoping to maintain this as long as I can
I feel the heat of you pressed into my back
Wanting to maintain the grounding it provides

I am safe
I am loved
I am rested

As I let this all sink in
The waggy tails stir
Beckoning me to them
Vocalising their excitement to start the day
So I am forced to break my morning reverie
I carefully extract myself from the bed
Taking a moment to enjoy your sleeping form
Smiling to myself
I shake the last remnants of sleep
Descending the stairs
I feel prepared to start the day

SERENITY

The afternoon sun glows brightly
Its rays lick at my cheeks
My skin soaks in the warmth greedily
I sit here in quiet contemplation
My pen poised above the paper
I close my eyes and inhale
Beneath my eyelids I see all my emotions
A spectrum of colours and sounds
My lips wrap around each of them
Ready to verbalise at will
Guiding my hand to form each line I write
As the last word is inked into the paper
I set down my pen
Take a deep breath, serene once more

COASTAL ADVENTURES

I sit here basking in the late light display
Remembering the jubilation of today
As we traversed the coastal delights
Up we walked, rose to lofty heights
The views breath-taking, set in a perfect frame
A landscape of calm, my eyes aflame
With a burning desire to soak in every detail
To map each rock, flower and sound along the trail
The babbling brook took us down to the cove
A chance to rest, enjoy the water on our toes
The waggy tails on point with each bird
That soared, over and around they whirred
With a look to the time, we made to leave
We resisted till the last, our hearts did grieve
Up the hill we trudged in slow time
Promising to return here to our slice of sublime

MINDFULNESS

I sit here in the shade as I write
My toes pulling gently at the lush green grass
Feeling it squish between each digit
The breeze wraps around me staving off the heat of the day
As I try to keep this English rose from wilting
Every once and a while a cool gust rushes my way, bouncing my curls
Tickling my flesh to form goose bumps
There isn't quite silence about me
I can hear the turning of the pages as my beautiful reads eagerly
I hear the gentle snores of the waggy tails as they lay at my feet
I hear the birds chittering and warbling
Such sweet melodies between the rustling sounds of the wind in the trees
The distant drone of the nearby road
Signals a connection to the outside world
I see the greens of the grass and trees
Complementing each other on their works of art
The cool blue of the sky showing the clouds in stunning relief
All fluffy and empty of the rain that was threatening earlier this morning

The smell of the open air, the grass, my herbal tea all infusing delightfully
As I take a bite of my lunch
My favourite sandwich my beautiful has made for me
I wonder to myself, how sublime life can be
I plan how I will take a slice of it home with me
To brighten those dark days when I find it difficult to shift my mood
To remind myself that
I can find happiness
I can entreat serenity
I can empty my head of negativity
I can exist in perfect harmony with everything around me
I am at one with myself
Comfortable in my own skin

THE COMFORT OF YOUR EMBRACE

I wake early, before the alarm
Ripped from sleep by the nightmares of my past and present
I panic as I realise I cannot feel your arms around me
As I slow my breaths, I hear your steady exhales from the pillow next to me
At once I feel the calm seep into me
You shift your arm, sensing what I need
I melt into you, clinging to you
Needing to feel grounded
Needing safety
Needing the warmth of your skin
I press my head to your chest
Your heartbeat strong and steady
Your embrace welcoming, enveloping all of me
I feel safe once more
In my favourite place with you
Knowing that you will kiss away the darkness in me

COMPETENCY

Today I have been assessed
Scrutinised
Measured up
Against the standards they've set
I have laid myself bare
To put my case forward
For why I deserve to be here
To be assigned the role
To lead
To drive forward
To manage change
To facilitate those corporate games
I painted a picture
Told my story
And answered their questions
In my honest way I told my truth
I explained my growth
I stated my case
I gave it my all
Now I await their judgement
On how a two hour window into my world
Convinces them that

I am resilient
I am courageous
I am valid
I am worthy
I am competent

AS LOVERS MEET AGAIN

It's the calm between the words
When all is said and done
The light and the dark
As the sun rise after night
The longing and the fulfilment
As lovers meet again
That is where you will find me
Between time
After night
Burnt forever in memory

THE CALM BETWEEN THE WORDS

It's the calm between the words
When the music has said and done
Gentle notes play between the sheets
As the melody meets the bridge
Slowly the notes unwind and chase
The end in tune, the music softens
Sheets of notes scatter across the floor
Resting in the hearth alight
The tempo fiery and strong
And beating to his rhythm
Again, the melody plays her part
Together in time, in tune, to the end
Now it's the calm between the words
When the music has said and done
Gentle notes play between the sheets
As sleep fills the silent night

SANCTUARY

I watched you sleep last night
Gentle breaths and sighs you took
Basking in the soft light of the moon
I traced the shape of you quietly
Soaking in every detail
Mapping the changes since we first met
Your beautiful face relaxed in slumber
Turning to me, somnolent
You invite me into your embrace
I fall into you
Resting in my favourite nook
Slipping into dreams of sanctuary with you

SKIN TO SKIN

I dream of you, skin to skin
Of pale and tan
Of silk and satin
Your touch light and true
My lips full of promise
Your eyes full of fire
My breath shallow
And as I trace your elegance
You open to me
My precious silk
My overwhelming desire
You come undone with me
We take a breath
We soak in the glory
You safe in my arms
Tonight, and for as long as you will want me
Our only promise to see what each new day brings

THE WHISPER OF YOUR VOICE

I feel the ghost of your hands
The way they mapped every part of me
I hear the whisper of your voice
The words that you kissed into my skin
I smell the essence of you
The heady scent still hangs in the room
I taste the sweetness of your love
The delicious nectar sustaining my love for you
I see the beauty of your face
The sun lighting your soul as you slumber beside me
I hope that you always choose me
I wish that happiness finds us both
I want this moment to last forever
I wait for you to awaken
Thinking of all the ways I will show you my love

A LITTLE THANK YOU

Your tender voice laps against my hollowed mind
Confusion-filled thoughts lay sleeping tonight
Those lilting tones send me to sleep at last

Waking from dreams of unforetold glories
Resonant fear is mellowed by the soft words you spoke
Whose gentle eyes quashed pain beneath each lid

Although pain still haunts my fragile existence
I am reminded by your words, who I am, who I was
You told me who I will be some day in time

I can only say thank you as no other words seem right
Your time though short brought me forward 100 years
Whilst your sense shone a light in a land of darkness

LET MY WORDS ROAM FREE

I woke early this morning
As the moon was still tracking across its arc
It's boldness shining a path for me in the pre-dawn sky
The waggy tails just as eager as me to start the day
I sit coffee in hand, my pen in the other and still my mind
Where does it want to take me today?
Will it be to the darkness, the sadness, the depths of my pain?
Or will it let me enumerate the happy, the colourful, the positivity
I can now create?
Sitting still, an achievement in itself
I begin the process of letting the nib hit the page
My hand moving of my minds accord
As I take a moment to study what I have written
My focus sharpens, the colours appear brighter
That is when I suddenly comprehend
It doesn't matter what I write about
I shouldn't force myself to write about one thing or another
As the subject doesn't matter
What does is that I write

I let the words flow free
I highlight my truths
I allow my honesty to take the lead
I refrain from censoring myself
I stop myself from only telling part of my story
It doesn't matter which way I construct the verse
I just need to let myself be free to express myself
So that the words become a healing balm for me
And the start of the journey for anyone who wishes to read my truths

DRIFTING TOWARDS SOMETHING NEW

I have found myself drifting recently
Unable to ground myself
My breakthroughs have shattered my anchors
And crumbled my foundations built on negativity
These had informed my self-perception
And directed my actions for decades
Keeping me locked into negative patterns
Making me compliant, a shadow of who I should be
Limiting me to a percentage of what I can achieve
I felt each anchor snap
The chains had groaned and cracked
As I had strained against them
The foundations rumbling with the force of me
As I stomped them down
The debris crushed to dust
It was then that I fell into the water
Felt it's coolness wash over me, cleanse me
The rush of the waves
Throwing me to the shore
Where the wind picked me up, taking me skywards
My arms outstretched waiting for the end...

...but that never came
The wind carried me like a leaf
Showing me every new possibility
Suggesting where I should build anew
Once it felt my acceptance
That I now held my destiny in the palm of my hand
It lowered me to a place between the old and the new
So I could walk some more with purpose
Decide where I wanted to start again
Laying new foundations built on my breakthroughs
I imbued them with
Positivity and Possibility
Self-love, Happiness and Courage
I created them with strength, fortitude and determination
Ensuring they would be fit for the warrior queen I have become

PATH TO FREEDOM

Last night the moon was full
With promises and delights
For the both of us
It shone my path to the rising sun

In between the rays of light
The darkness swallowed
And sucked away the purity
It left the earth lifeless, empty

I watched the moon closely
As it held me in high regard
But mocked my choices
It shone my righteous path to freedom

Last night the moon was full
As I walked my path to freedom
Away from you
It led to the rising sun

FINDING MY IDENTITY

All at once I had what I wanted
The freedom of being myself
A burgeoning romance
So why was it all still a struggle?
Why did navigating my truth weigh heavy on me?
I thought the reveal would be the most difficult
But this wasn't the case
Of course there were losses
People who left along the way
Those who couldn't understand me
However, what was most challenging was how I viewed myself
How I thought people viewed me
My life long obsession with needing to conform
Needing to prove that this wasn't a phase, a pre-mid life blip
I set about reframing my identity
The hair, the clothes
Finding a new love in colours and plaid and boyfriend fit

I needed to prove this was me
Needed to bury the old me
The party girl with the short hemline would be no more
I was trying to create a new identity to fit my new life
My true life
But what I forgot was the essence of me
That I didn't need to posit myself as this or that
I didn't need to code myself
I just needed to let myself be me
I just needed to let everybody see
Because this is where my truth is

WHISPERS AND REMEMBRANCE

I hate seeing you marked this way
You whisper as you kiss me reverently
Those healing lips brushing ever so softly
Across the deep purple that tarnishes my shoulder
I turn towards you, eyes bright
Knowing this conversation will always be repeated
They are my periapts, I whisper
As if my voice will break their spells
I wear these with pride
In the knowledge that now I can protect myself
That I am stronger than ever
I wear these to remind myself of the times when I was over powered
Of when I wasn't strong enough
I know that you understand
That you only ask so that I can remind myself
So I can whisper my affirmations
Of strength, fortitude and determination
Embedding them into my skin until it sparkles
The periapts fading until my next training session
Leaving me with the confidence that
I am a Warrior Queen

WORDS FROM YOUR CHEERLEADER

Remember that you are amazing, strong, resilient, brave, caring, supportive, confident and many more wonderful things
But most of all you are kind and sometimes we forget to be kind to ourselves
So forgive yourself when you don't quite achieve what you wanted
Give yourself a break when you have those times that it all gets too much
Keep close the people who support you in everything you do, even when you are at your lowest
Remember that none of us have all the answers to everything, sometimes we are just winging it hoping nobody will notice
Re-read this whenever you need to and remember that everything I have said is true
Because I see you!
And for every negative you may see in yourself
I can give you twice as many positives that I witness in everything you do!

www.ingramcontent.com/pod-product-compliance
Lightning Source LLC
Chambersburg PA
CBHW061211070526
44583CB00025B/3211